RUDOLF STEINER (1861–1925) called his spiritual philosophy 'anthroposophy', which can be understood as 'wisdom of the human being'. A highly developed seer, Steiner based his work on direct knowledge and perception of spiritual dimensions. He initiated a modern and universal 'science of spirit', accessible to anybody willing to exercise clear and unprejudiced thinking.

From his spiritual investigations, Steiner provided suggestions for the renewal of many activities, including education—both general and special—agriculture, medicine, economics, architecture, science, philosophy, religion and the arts. Today there are literally thousands of schools, clinics, farms and other organizations doing practical work based on his principles. His many published works (writings and lectures) also feature his research into the spiritual nature of the human being, the evolution of the world and humanity, and methods of personal development. Steiner wrote some 30 books and delivered over 6,000 lectures across Europe. In 1924 he founded the General Anthroposophical Society, which today has branches throughout the world.

Also in the *Meditations* series:

Meditations for Times of Day and Seasons of the Year, Breathing the Spirit

Meditations for Courage and Tranquillity, The Heart of Peace

Meditations for the Dead, Connecting to those who have Died

MEDITATIONS
for Harmony and Healing

Finding the Greater Self

Rudolf Steiner

Edited and translated
by Matthew Barton

Sophia Books

An imprint of Rudolf Steiner Press

Sophia Books
An imprint of Rudolf Steiner Press
Hillside House, The Square
Forest Row, East Sussex
RH18 5ES

www.rudolfsteinerpress.com

Published by Rudolf Steiner Press 2002
New edition 2018

Rudolf Steiner's verses are selected from the following volumes of the *Rudolf Steiner Gesamtausgabe* ('GA'), his Collected Works published in the original German by Rudolf Steiner Verlag, Dornach: GA 40 *Wahrspruchworte*, GA 267 *Seelenübungen* and GA 268 *Mantrische Sprüche*. This authorized volume is published by permission of the Rudolf Steiner Nachlassverwaltung, Dornach

This selection and translation © Rudolf Steiner Press 2002

All rights reserved. No part of this publication may be reproduced, stored in a retrieval system, or transmitted, in any form or by any means, electronic, mechanical, photocopying or otherwise, without the prior permission of the publishers

A catalogue record for this book is available from the British Library

ISBN 978 1 85584 549 7

Typeset by DP Photosetting, Aylesbury, Bucks.
Printed and bound in Great Britain by 4Edge Ltd., Essex

Contents

Introduction	7
FINDING THE GREATER SELF	9
Notes	69
Index of first lines	71

*Man, you are the condensed, compressed
image of the world.
World you are the being of man
poured out into far expanse.*

Introduction

One of Rudolf Steiner's great and enduring gifts to us was to show, in great and specific detail, how we are intimately linked with the wider world around us: how, in fact, we can only really know and understand ourselves by looking out into the substances and processes at work in the cosmos; and only know the world by looking into the microcosmic depths of the human self. He returned to this theme again and again, unfolding worlds of interconnection that can give us modern human beings, increasingly sundered from a living relationship with nature, a renewed sense of our true place in the greater scheme of things.

The verses gathered here all relate to this theme in some way, and repeatedly focus on the relationship between spirit and matter, on ways in which we can integrate these two aspects in ourselves, and heal the divisions within and between us.

Just by being here, alive on earth, we continually encounter riddles and problems which, as Steiner says, we can only solve by living. These meditations aim to help us bring the riddles into sharper focus and offer the beginnings of answers only we ourselves can ultimately provide.

Matthew Barton

FINDING THE GREATER SELF

When man knows himself,
self becomes world;
when man knows the world,
world becomes self.

Up from world depths, mysteriously
matter's rich fullness springs, impresses
itself upon our human senses;
and down from world heights streams
into the ground of the soul
spirit's full, clarifying word.
Meeting within the human being
they merge in wise reality.

If you wish to know yourself,
seek yourself in the world's far breadths;
if you wish to know the world,
penetrate your inner depths.
Your own depths will disclose,
as in world memory,
the mysteries of the cosmos to you.

When man found how the world
endlessly fragments in atoms,
his perception bound itself
with the death of nature;
now he should strive in spirit
to find what ends fragmentation
and then his gaze will turn
to the world's evolving growth.[1]

The riddles of life resolve
in the warmth of a heart that strives
towards the light of thought.

Receiving oneself from world existence,
experiencing the world as your self's being—
that is the path to the goal of true vision.

Never speak of the limits to human knowledge, only of the limits to your own.

We only see clearly in the outer world
what we can illumine through the light within.[2]

The love of supersensible realms transforms
the ore of science into wisdom's gold.

In the heart
feeling weaves,

in the head
thinking shines,

in the limbs
will's forceful strength.

Weaving light,
strong weaving,
shining strength:
this is man.

As I walk
I overcome earth's weight;

in my gaze
I bear human spirit;

in my heart
springs the strength of the sun;

in my breath
lives the power of the soul;

in the breezes blow
God's creative force;

In the stars works
spirit's world-conquering light;

So I think and feel and will
through time and eternity.

We must ponder on
the riddle of the world;
yet it will not be solved
through idea or word.
Look on the human soul:
itself the answer.

The riddles of the soul will not
be solved by dwelling in mere sense light;
those who wish to comprehend life
must strive upwards to the spirit's heights!

In the unbounded outer world
find yourself as human being,
in narrow, contracted inner life
feel worlds spread boundlessly;
then veils will fall away, and show
that the solution to the riddle of the world
is nought else but man.

In life, soul learns to think; and thinks
all creatures that compose sense being.
Yet when it feels truly vigorous, the soul
does not just learn to know itself through
 thinking.
For then soul knows that gods are thinking it
in the far-flung universe!

World knowledge, self-knowledge:
soul longing swings from one to other.
Often a solution to its conundrums
seems to offer comfort, but the next
swing of the pendulum makes of one
solution just another riddle.
Yet if, instead of looking outwards
to understand depths of existence,
and instead of self-reflection
on the human being's eternal core,
selfhood is sought in world breadths
and the universe in the self,
then soul longing—while not attaining
its ultimate goal—finds paths that open
into knowledge: soul-sustaining,
spirit-lifting, world-directing.

You seek
for the light of the spirit world:
seek within yourself
and you will find it.

You seek
for your self's being:
seek in world unfolding
and you will find it.

Our own being's darkness
darkens the world.
Not to know the workings of the world
chills the self.

When the human being, warm in love,
gives himself to the world as soul,
when the human being, lucid in thinking,
takes spirit from the world:
then in spirit-lit soul,
in soul-born spirit,
human spirit in human body
will truly manifest.

The human being is a stage where the eternal and
   the transient meet—
his perception experiences the eternal, for which
   he himself is an organ of perception—
his deeds are the deeds of eternity, which he
   himself only mediates—

so understand this:

You are the eye of the primal spirit—
    through you he sees his creating.
You are the hand of the primal spirit—
    through you he forms his creation.

In the heart
there lives a part of man
that contains substance which
is most spiritual of all;
that lives as spirit manifesting
most materially.

That is why the sun
is the heart in the human cosmos;
that is why in the heart
the human being finds his being's
deepest source.

I see
a small sun in
my heart;
the small sun
shines through my body;
I feel it warm
within me.

In my heart
the sun's strength streams,
in my soul
the world's warmth works.

I will breathe
the strength of the sun.

I will feel
the warmth of the world.

Sun strength fills me,
world warmth penetrates me.

I look into the dark:
within it arises light,
living light.
Who is this light in the dark?
I am it myself in my reality,
This reality of the I
does not enter my earthly life.
I am only an image of it.
But I will find it once again
when, with good will for the spirit,
I have passed beyond death's gate.

Into the eye of man
shines the sun from world heights.
Into human senses
shimmer beings from breadths of space.
The human heart thirsts
to unite itself with spirit.

Look at the plant:
earth-bound butterfly.

Look at the butterfly:
cosmos-freed plant.

Salt crystal:
dissolving in water,
the colour coming alive,
unfolding into a lily,
from which a white butterfly rises,
flies to the thinking spirit beings
in the cosmos.

I will join my soul knowledge
to the fire of blossom scent;

I will rouse my soul life
at the glittering drops
of morning's leaves;

I will strengthen my soul being
through salt's condensing force, with which
earth carefully nurtures roots.

The plants live in
sunlight's strength,
the bodies of human beings
work in soul-light's power;
and what sun's heavenly light
is to the plant,
so to the human body
is spirit's soul-light.

In seed-form we bear
the future of worlds
when we turn the sense of our deeds
into strength of thought
and through the eye of thought
gazes spirit sun's strength.

The seed of truth lies in love;
seek love's root in truth—
your higher self says this.

Fire's ardour turns wood into warmth,
the will set loose by knowledge turns work into
   strength.

Let your work be the shadow cast by your I
when lit by the flame of your higher self.

Without belief, work stays dead:
belief ignites work's breath and bears it
upwards into ethereal heights,
sucks in work's breath and offers it
as becoming's sacrifice to being.

The I is the core and centre of all life,
in it merge the workings of all beings.
In the I moves all primordial life,
in it rests all future growth.
Saturn will anchors I's inwardness,
Sun life propels the inner changing image,
Moon soul forms the waves of life,
Mars tempers the power of the will,
Mercury plunges into the sea of existence,
Jupiter gives number, measure, weight;
and then, Venus may bring love.

The I is all beings,
all beings are the I.

The I receives all beings made manifest,
all beings made manifest stream from the I.

The I contains the effects of all beings,
the effect of all beings is overcome by the I.

The I is born from effects overcome,
effects overcome free themselves from the I.

In the universe
essence of the human being weaves;
in the core of man
reflection of worlds holds sway.
The I joins both together
and thus creates
life's true sense and purpose.

The cosmos holds watch
the sphere of heaven dreams
the world of planets sleeps
the earth being rests.

In resting man wakes,
in sleeping man feels
in dreaming man wills
in waking man is I

I am I—I am
I will—I pass away
I feel—I become
I think—I am not—it is.

Seek the truly practical, material life—
but seek it so that it does not numb you
to the spirit that is active in it.

Seek the spirit—
but do not seek it in supersensible lust,
out of supersensible egotism;
no, seek it
because you wish to apply it selflessly
in practical life in the material world.

Keep to the old principle:
'Spirit is never without matter, matter is never
without spirit', in such a way that you say:
Let us do everything material in the light of spirit,
let us seek the light of the spirit
so that it unfolds warmth for our practical deeds.

Building the world in the I,
seeing the I in worlds,
is soul breath.

Experiencing the whole cosmos
in self-sensing
is wisdom's pulse.

And inscribing spirit's paths
into one's own aims
is truth's language.

Let soul breath penetrate
into wisdom's pulse, delivering
from human depths
truth's language into
year-rhythms of life.[3]

In primeval times
the spirit of earth
came to the spirit of heaven,
and asked:
Will you endow me with the language
through which the world heart
knows how to speak to the human heart?
Then the heaven spirit gave to the earth spirit: art.

The link with spirit is sundered
if not sustained by beauty.
Beauty links I to body.

We are a bridge
between our past
and future existence;
The present a moment,
the moment as bridge.
Spirit grown soul
in matter's enveloping sheath
comes from the past;
soul growing to spirit
in germinal spheres
is our future path.
Take hold of the future
through the past,
hope for what's coming
through what became.
So grasp existence
through growth; so grasp
what's growing in what exists.

Feeling the breath—gentle feeling

Within me lifts world-wave strength
on the waves lives will of gods,
will of gods you fill me full,
I enliven you to human will,
within the human will my being itself
becomes full strength-creating life;
I work out of the I into the world.

Feeling the blood's circulation—gentle hearing

Within me calms the power of human will,
in the calm lives human thinking,
human thinking, you illumine me,
I grasp hold of you as thoughts of God,
in God thoughts rests my archetypal being,
and archetypal being creates light in me;
I think from God into the I.

High spirits who were perfected
before the spring of our beginning flowed,
your creative wisdom formed the world,
and from your world wisdom rose

>   strength of our thinking,
>   life of our feeling,
>   aim of our will.

May your strength, your life, your aim
pour into active structures of our soul,
so that they see your creative wisdom,
so that they live creative feeling,
so that they create within divine will.

You human self, perceiving, feeling, willing—
you are the riddle of the world;
what the world hides is made
manifest in you, becomes
light in your spirit, warmth in your soul;
and your strength of breath
joins your bodily being
to soul worlds,
to spirit realms.
It leads you into matter
so that you find yourself human;
it leads you into spirit
so that you do not lose your spiritual self.

The sphere of the spirit is the soul's true home;
and we human beings reach that sphere
when we tread true thinking's path,
when we choose the power of heart's love
to lead and guide us well,
and when we open our inner sense of soul
to the script which everywhere
is manifest in world being,
which we can always find
as spirit annunciation
in all that lives and works,
as well as in all things
spread round us lifeless in the spatial world,
and in everything that happens
in the evolving stream of time.

In workings of earth draw close to me,
given me in matter's reflected image,
the heavenly beings of stars: within my will
I see them lovingly transform themselves.

    I experience myself as soul.

In fluid life there enter into me,
forming me in matter's force and strength,
the heavenly deeds of stars: within my feeling
I see their wise transforming of themselves.

    I experience myself as spirit.

In the beginning was the Word,
may the Word be in me,
may the Word work in me,
may the Word bear me
into spirit worlds,
into depths of soul.

May my soul raise itself
up to world breadths,
may my soul deepen itself
in depths of heart;
and seek to experience
world breadths
in depths of heart.

Whoever denies the world spirit does not know that he denies himself. Such a one does not merely make a mistake, but fails in his chief task: to work out of the spirit.

Four pillars of wisdom

In pure thinking you will find
the self that can sustain itself.

By transforming thought to image,
experience living, creating wisdom.

Condensing feeling into light,
you reveal forming strength.

By embodying will in being,
you create in world existence.

Great, sublime spirit
who fills the world's far expanse,
who plunges into grounds of soul,
fill this our place of work,
fill our seeking souls,
strengthen our will,
warm our thinking,
cleanse our thinking
now and forever.

In my thinking world thoughts live,
in my feeling world powers weave,
in my will, will beings work.

> I will perceive myself
>   In world thoughts,
> I will experience myself
>   In world powers
> I will create myself
>   In beings of will

So I will not end at world ends
nor in breadths of space.
I begin at world ends
and in breadths of space;
> and only end with myself
> perceiving myself within me.

Learn to be silent and power shall come to you.
Give yourself up to power and will shall come to you.
Give yourself up to will and feeling shall come to you.
Give yourself up to feeling and knowledge shall come to you.

From the spirit's light-filled heights
may God's clear, bright light ray out
into human souls
who wish to seek
spirit's grace,
spirit's strength,
spirit's being.

May it live
in the heart,
in the inner soul,
of us who feel ourselves gathered here
in the spirit's name.

May our feeling
penetrate the heart's deep core
and seek to join in love
with those who share our aims,
with spirits who full of grace
look down from
regions of light upon
our earnest, heartfelt striving
strengthening us,
brightening our love.

Devotion to matter
means crushing souls.

Meeting in spirit
means joining human beings.

Seeing ourselves in the human being
means building worlds.

We can only gain true self-knowledge
by developing loving interest in others;
we can only gain true knowledge of the world
by trying to understand our own being.

Health and wholesomeness only come
when in the mirror of the soul of man
the whole community takes shape;
and in the community lives
the strength of every single soul.[4]

Observe the pendulum swinging
between self and the world:
to you will be revealed
human-world-being,
world-human being.

Notes

[1] Given to Edith Maryon.
[2] Given to a painter.
[3] Given to Marie Steiner.
[4] Given to Edith Maryon.

Index of first lines

As I walk I overcome earth's weight, 21
Building the world in the I, 46
Devotion to matter, 65
From the spirit's light-filled heights, 63
Great, sublime spirit, 60
Health and wholesomeness only come, 67
High spirits who were perfected, 52
If you wish to know yourself, 13
I look into the dark, 33
In life, soul learns to think, 25
In my heart the sun's strength streams, 32
In my thinking world thoughts live, 61
In primeval times, 47
In pure thinking you will find, 59
In seed-form we bear, 39
In the beginning was the Word, 56
In the heart feeling weaves, 20
In the heart there lives a part of man, 30
In the unbounded outer world, 24
In the universe essence of the human being weaves, 43
Into the eye of man, 34
In workings of earth draw close to me, 55
I see a small sun in my heart, 31
I will join my soul knowledge, 37
Learn to be silent and power shall come to you, 62
Look at the plant, 35

Man you are the condensed, compressed, 6
May my soul raise itself, 57
May our feeling penetrate the heart's deep core, 64
Never speak of the limits to human knowledge, 17
Observe the pendulum swinging, 68
Receiving oneself from world existence, 16
Salt crystal: dissolving in water, 36
Seek the truly practical, material life, 45
The cosmos holds watch, 44
The human being is a stage where the eternal and the transient meet, 29
The I is all beings, 42
The I is the core and centre of all life, 41
The link with spirit is sundered, 48
The love of supersensible realms transforms, 19
The plants live in sunlight's strength, 38
The riddles of life resolve, 15
The riddles of the soul will not, 23
The seed of truth lies in love, 40
The sphere of the spirit is the soul's true home, 54
Up from world depths, mysteriously, 12
We are a bridge between our past, 49
We can only gain true self-knowledge, 66
We must ponder on, 22
We only see clearly in the outer world, 18
When man found how the world, 14
When man knows himself, 11
When the human being, warm in love, 28
Whoever denies the world spirit does not know, 58

Within me calms the power of human will, 51
Within me lifts world-wave strength, 50
World knowledge, self-knowledge, 26
You human self, perceiving, feeling, willing, 53
You seek for the light of the spirit world, 27